The Rosary of the Virgin Mary

Cover design: Blair Turner
Layout: Blair Turner and Blaine Herrmann
Illustrations: Benoît Mercier
Editorial texts: Most Rev. Raymond J. Lahey

Business Office:
Novalis
49 Front Street East, 2nd Floor
Toronto, Ontario, Canada M5E 1B3
Phone: 1-877-702-7773 or (416) 363-3303
Fax: 1-877-702-7775 or (416) 363-9409
E-mail: cservice@novalis.ca
www.novalis.ca

ISBN: 2-89507-452-6 (book)
2-89507-463-1 (book plus rosary)

Canadian Cataloguing in Publication: C2003-905340-7

Printed in Canada.

We acknowledge the financial support of the Government of Canada through the Book Publishing Industry Development Program (BPIDP) for our publishing activities.

10 9 8 7 6 5 4 3 2 1 07 06 05 04 03

Contents

Introduction

On October 16, 2002, the day he began the twenty-fifth year of his pontificate, Pope John Paul II addressed to the whole Church an Apostolic Letter called *Rosarium Virginis Mariae* (The Rosary of the Virgin Mary). Writing on a devotion that is obviously dear to him, he offers the Church a reflection that continues the theme of inviting the People of God to "start afresh from Christ," a theme he had set forth in an earlier letter, *Novo Millennio Ineunte* (At the Beginning of a New Millennium).

In his letter on the Rosary, Pope John Paul II

- proclaimed October 2002–October 2003 the "Year of the Rosary"
- described the Rosary as "Learning Christ from Mary"
- underlined the fact that the Rosary is a listening to the Scriptures
- announced five new mysteries: "The Mysteries of Light"
- suggested changes to the way the Rosary is prayed.

A Brief History of the Rosary

Although his letter contains several references to the history of the Rosary, John Paul II did not attempt to cover this topic in detail, perhaps because its development is complex and sometimes uncertain. However, a brief overview may be helpful here.

While it is often attributed to St. Dominic (1170–1221), the Rosary ("crown of roses") as we know it evolved gradually in the later Middle Ages, especially under Dominican and Cistercian influence. Its development paralleled somewhat the development of the *Hail Mary*, which is central to the Rosary. Although the *Ave Maria* is recorded as a prayer from much earlier times, and its opening is taken directly from the Scriptures, its last part did not come into use until the later 1400s.

The Rosary emerged as a short substitute for the Divine Office for the laity to use: 150 *Aves* replaced the 150 Psalms. This devotion of saying the 150 *Aves* daily was certainly known even before St. Dominic, as was the practice of counting prayers on beads or knotted strings. Apparently in the fourteenth century, the Aves were divided into decades (groups of 10), which began with an *Our Father*. Shortly afterwards arose the custom of attaching particular thoughts about the lives of Mary or Jesus to the 50 or 150 Aves.

The popularity of the Rosary is closely connected to Alan de Rupe (Alain de la Roche; c. 1428–1475), a Dominican friar who founded Confraternities of the Holy Rosary. In the early 1500s, the practice of separate "*Hail Mary* thoughts" gradually died out, giving way instead to brief "*Our Father* thoughts," which we know today as the "mysteries" of the Rosary. The Rosary also owes much to Pope St. Pius V. It was he who standardized the fifteen traditional mysteries in 1569. In 1571, in thanksgiving for the victory of the Christian forces at the battle of Lepanto, he instituted the feast of the Holy Rosary (October 7), which later became a feast of the universal Church.

In more recent years, in adapted form, the Rosary has sometimes become an ecumenical form of prayer. Indeed, a respected Protestant theologian welcomed Pope John Paul II's document, calling it "a letter of a spiritual and theological depth that I wasn't expecting—a letter that breathes an evangelical dimension."[1]

While it gives no history of the Rosary as such, the papal letter does refer to several more modern figures who promoted the Rosary, including St. Louis de Montfort (1673–1716), who taught devotion to Mary as a way of becoming configured to Christ; St. Padre Pio (1887–1968); and Blessed Bartolo Longo (1841–1926), a married layman whom John Paul II credited with promoting the Christ-centred and contemplative heart of the Rosary. The letter also repeats the well-known saying of Father Patrick Peyton, csc (1909–1992), founder of the Family Rosary Crusade: "The family that prays together, stays together." The Pope himself firmly believes in the power of the Rosary, as he states at the opening of his letter: "Simple yet profound, it still remains, at the dawn of this third millennium, a prayer of great significance."

The Year of the Rosary

John Paul II begins his letter by proclaiming October 2002–October 2003 the "Year of the Rosary," and asks that during this period the Rosary be especially emphasized and promoted according to the particular circumstances of each community. "The Rosary," he explains, "reclaimed in its full meaning, goes to the very heart of Christian life; it offers familiar yet fruitful spiritual and educational opportunity for personal contemplation, the formation of the People of God, and the new evangelization."

In his letter, he describes the Rosary as a very basic means of fostering prayer. It is a commitment to the contemplation of the Christian mystery, a form of "training in holiness." "To recite the Rosary," he adds, "is nothing other than to contemplate with Mary the face of Christ." In this way, the Rosary is a prayer that both sustains the liturgy of the Church and is directed to the very centre of Christian faith, Christ himself.

Learning Christ from Mary

Calling Christ "the supreme Teacher, the revealer and the one revealed," the Pope continues: "It is not just a question of learning what he taught but of *'learning him.'*" He then asks: "In this regard, could we have any better teacher than Mary?" No one, he points out, knows Christ better than Mary.

The Rosary, therefore, is a way of learning Christ from Mary. When we pray the Rosary, each of its mysteries leads us to look in a different way at the face of Christ through Mary's eyes. Quoting Pope Paul VI (1963–1978), John Paul II repeats that the Rosary is not a matter of multiplying words, but of providing a quiet rhythm and a lingering pace to allow us to meditate on the mysteries of the Lord. These mysteries belong to "the 'today' of salvation," he reminds us. "If Jesus, the one Mediator, is the Way of our prayer," he adds, "then Mary, his purest and most transparent reflection, shows us the Way."

By learning Christ from Mary, the Pope tells us, we are conformed to Christ with her, we pray to him with her, and finally we proclaim him with her. This is a wonderful catechetical opportunity, "a prayerful and contemplative presentation, capable of forming Christians according to the heart of Christ."

"The Mysteries of Light": Reflecting the Scriptures More Fully

In his letter, Pope John Paul II calls the Rosary as we know it "a compendium of the Gospel": a reflection on Christ's Incarnation, his Passion, and the triumph of his Resurrection. However, he notes that its mysteries neither replace the Gospel nor exhaust its contents; the Rosary is not a substitute for the Word of God, but presupposes and promotes the practice of reading from Scripture. To underline this point, he expressly asks that each mystery begin with a Scripture reading.

To more fully include the whole Gospel message in the Rosary, John Paul II added five new mysteries to the traditional fifteen. These "Mysteries of Light,"[2] which recount Christ's public ministry, remember Christ as the Light of the world:

1. The Baptism of Jesus in the Jordan
2. The Wedding Feast at Cana
3. The Proclamation of the Kingdom of God
4. The Transfiguration
5. The Institution of the Eucharist.

These new mysteries deal with the "epiphany" (manifestation) of Jesus, his self-revelation as the Christ and the Lord, the beloved Son from whom the glory of the Godhead shines forth. In this they recall that Christ himself is the sacrament of God's new covenant with us, and further recall the sacraments in which we encounter him: Baptism, Marriage, Reconciliation (the Proclamation of the Kingdom with its call to repentance), and the Eucharist. The mystery of the

Transfiguration reinforces this theme, reminding us of our own transformation in Christ through the sacraments, beginning in Baptism. In these Mysteries of Light, says the Pope, the words of Mary at Cana—"Do whatever he tells you" (John 2:5), which echo the very command of God, "Listen to him" (Luke 9:35)—speak to every age.[3]

Prayer for Peace and Family Prayer

John Paul II ends his letter on the Rosary by speaking of it as "a sweet chain linking us to God": a great prayer for world peace and a wonderful form of family prayer. In his view, no one can look upon the face of Christ as presented in the Rosary without acknowledging the need to see the face of Christ in others, especially in the world's most afflicted. "By focusing our eyes on Christ," he says, "the Rosary also makes us peacemakers in the world." It is not a form of escape from the world's problems, he tells us; on the contrary, it "obliges us to see them with responsible and generous eyes."

He strongly urges every family to pray the Rosary, which is particularly effective in family prayer. By praying the Rosary for and with their children, especially when it is prayed in the way he suggests above, parents bring their children to know Christ. To make the Rosary more accessible to children, he encourages parents to use symbols and other practical aids—pictures or icons would certainly be appropriate—to help them follow along.

Recognizing the challenges of contemporary society and family life, the Pope suggests that the family Rosary can be a way of "filling daily life with very different images.... In turning their eyes toward Jesus, [family members] also regain the ability to look one another in the eye, to communicate, to show solidarity, to forgive one another." At the end of his letter, John Paul II describes the Rosary as a treasure waiting to be rediscovered by the Christian community. In his words, "Why not try it?"

Praying the Rosary

In his letter on the Rosary, Pope John Paul II tells us that to be faithful to the spirit of the Rosary, we must make sure we pray it with care, especially in public. Although he recognizes the freedom of people to pray it as they see fit, he also offers some concrete suggestions about how to pray the Rosary. He reminds us that it always ought to be not just words, but a true contemplation of Christ and a meditation on his mysteries.

Even the Rosary beads, he says, are not just a simple counting mechanism, but something symbolic, "a sweet chain which unites us to God." The beads converge upon the crucifix, reminding us that the prayer of believers is always centred upon Christ: "Everything begins from him, everything leads towards him, everything, through him, in the Holy Spirit, attains to the Father."

The Mysteries Spread Throughout the Week

In order to respect the Christ-centred nature of the Rosary, Catholics might change how they pray the Rosary. First, to include the new Mysteries of Light, the mysteries would be rearranged and prayed on the days listed:

- The Joyful Mysteries (Mysteries of Joy)—on Mondays and Saturdays
- The Mysteries of Light—on Thursdays
- The Sorrowful Mysteries (Mysteries of Sorrow)—on Tuesdays and Fridays
- The Glorious Mysteries (Mysteries of Glory)—on Wednesdays and Sundays

The Beginning of the Rosary

The Rosary could begin in one of two ways:

- with the simple verse and response from Psalm 70, without the Sign of the Cross or the Creed:

  V. **God, come to my assistance.**
  R. **Lord, make haste to help me.**

or

- with the Sign of the Cross and then the Apostles' Creed:
  In the name of the Father, and of the Son, and of the Holy Spirit. Amen.

I believe in God, the Father almighty, creator of heaven and earth.

I believe in Jesus Christ, his only Son, our Lord. He was conceived by the power of the Holy Spirit and born of the Virgin Mary. He suffered under Pontius Pilate, was crucified, died, and was buried. He descended to the dead. On the third day he rose again. He ascended into heaven, and is seated at the right hand of the Father. He will come again to judge the living and the dead.

I believe in the Holy Spirit, the holy catholic Church, the communion of saints, the forgiveness of sins, the resurrection of the body, and the life everlasting. Amen.

Although it has often been the practice to follow the *Creed* with the *Our Father,* three *Hail Marys* (the first evoking faith; the second, hope; and the third, charity) and the *Glory to the Father*, this is a more recent addition to the Rosary. The papal letter does not refer to this custom, perhaps because it does not relate to the central focus of the Rosary, which is the unfolding of the mysteries of Christ. These prayers may be omitted. If they are used, the expanded form of the *Hail Mary* (mentioning the theme of the mystery after Jesus' name) would not be used, since this form is intended to focus on a particular mystery of Christ.

Praying Each Decade

To make the Rosary a means of contemplation, and to recall its Scriptural roots, the Pope calls for each decade to be introduced as follows:

- The announcement of the particular mystery, perhaps accompanied by an icon to portray it.
- A reading of the Word of God. [Shorter readings are designed for personal use. Longer ones are especially suitable for public recitation. Appropriate readings are given in this book.]
- A brief period of silent reflection.

Each decade would continue as usual, beginning with the Our Father:

Our Father, who art in heaven, hallowed be thy name; thy kingdom come; thy will be done on earth as it is in heaven. Give us this day our daily bread; and forgive us our trespasses as we forgive those who trespass against us; and lead us not into temptation, but deliver us from evil. Amen.[4]

For each decade, the *Hail Mary* is prayed ten times. In a public recitation, it is often begun by an individual and concluded by all present. To recognize both the mystery celebrated and the central place of Jesus, John Paul II suggests mentioning the theme of the mystery after the name of Jesus, "the centre of gravity" in each *Hail Mary*, especially when the Rosary is prayed publicly. This can be done quite easily when the decade is led by a person who says the first part of the *Hail Mary*. For example, the second sorrowful mystery would proclaim, "… and blessed is the fruit of your womb, Jesus, by whose wounds we are healed. Holy Mary, Mother of God …" [Appropriate phrases for each mystery are provided in this book.]

> **Hail Mary, full of grace, the Lord is with you. Blessed are you among women and blessed is the fruit of your womb, Jesus …**
> [*Here a phrase appropriate to each mystery may be inserted.*]
> **Holy Mary, Mother of God, pray for us sinners,**
> **now and at the hour of our death. Amen.**

At the end of each decade comes the *Glory to the Father*. Because this prayer is the acclamation of praise of the Holy Trinity and thus the high point of the decade, the Pope suggests that it should be sung, especially when the Rosary is prayed publicly. Many simple chants are available for this prayer of praise. The following may be freely reproduced for distribution without charge, provided proper attribution is given:

Glory to the Father

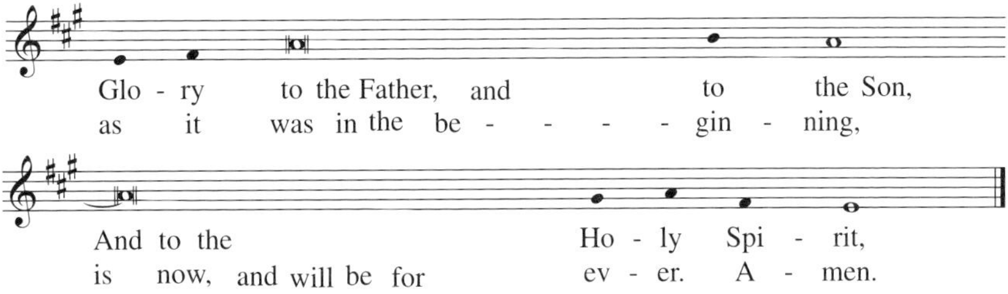

Text: traditional Latin doxology

This is the approved form from the liturgy of the Church.

He also addresses the short prayer that is commonly said after each decade. While he is no doubt familiar with the Fatima prayer ("O my Jesus..."), the Pope certainly does not feel that it is required, since he does not mention it at all. In fact, although he says that he does not want to diminish "a legitimate variety of forms," he suggests instead using a prayer of a quite different kind. Saying that the truly appropriate prayer after each decade would be one that prays for the fruits of the mystery and connects the mystery to the Christian life, he proposes as an example a prayer from the liturgical tradition of the Church:

> **O God, whose only begotten Son, by his life, death, and resurrection, has purchased for us the rewards of eternal life, grant, we beseech you, that meditating upon this mystery of** [*insert the title of the particular mystery just prayed*] **we may imitate what it contains and obtain what it promises, through the same Christ Our Lord. Amen.**

Alternatively, the following prayer[5] may be said after each decade of the Joyful Mysteries:

Lord our God, through the Blessed Virgin Mary you revealed your Son to the world as the glory of Israel and the light of all the nations. Grant that as we follow his teaching and example we may strengthen our faith in Christ, and acknowledge him to be the one mediator and the Saviour of the world. We make our prayer through Christ our Lord. Amen.

The following prayer[6] may be said after each decade of the Mysteries of Light:

All holy Father, in your divine wisdom and love you chose that the Blessed Virgin Mary should play her part in the mysteries of our salvation. Grant that by heeding her words, we may do what he commands us in the Gospel he has given us. We ask this through Christ our Lord. Amen.

The following prayer[7] may be said after each decade of the Sorrowful Mysteries:

God of mercies, your only Son, while hanging on the cross, appointed the Blessed Virgin Mary, his mother, to be our mother also. Like her, and under her loving care, may your

Church grow day by day, rejoice in the holiness of its children, and so attract to itself all the peoples of the earth, through Christ our Lord. Amen.

The following prayer[8] may be said after each decade of the Glorious Mysteries:

Lord our God, you chose the Blessed Virgin, formed by the Holy Spirit, as the first fruits of the new creation. Grant that we may reject the old ways of sin, embrace wholeheartedly the new life of the Gospel, and honour faithfully the new commandment of love, through Christ our Lord. Amen.

Other prayers that are suitable to the mysteries being celebrated and that pray for the fruits of the mystery might also be considered.

The Pope then refers to the opening and closing prayers of the Rosary. He notes that both the use of the invocation and response from Psalm 70 ("*God, come to my assistance. / Lord, make haste to help me*") and the recitation of the Creed are equally legitimate ways of beginning the Rosary. He makes no reference to an opening *Our Father*, three *Hail Marys* and a *Glory to the Father*, which were later additions to the Rosary.

Concluding the Rosary

To keep in mind the needs of the whole Church, the papal letter on the Rosary asks that the Rosary be concluded at the end of the five decades by a prayer for the Pope's intentions, such as

> **Let us pray for the intentions of our Holy Father, the Pope, especially for his intention for this month,**
> **for...** [Name the Pope's monthly intention and pause for brief silent prayer.][9]
> **We pray to the Lord:**
> R. **Lord, hear our prayer.**

Either the *Litany of Loreto* (p. 76) or, more commonly, the *Salve Regina* ("Hail, Holy Queen") closes the Rosary. Especially in public recitation, this hymn might properly be sung, either in Latin (*Catholic Book of Worship* III, #469) or in the English version, "Hail, Holy Queen Enthroned Above" (*Catholic Book of Worship* III, #457).

The following versions may be freely reproduced for distribution without charge, provided proper attribution is given:

Salve Regina

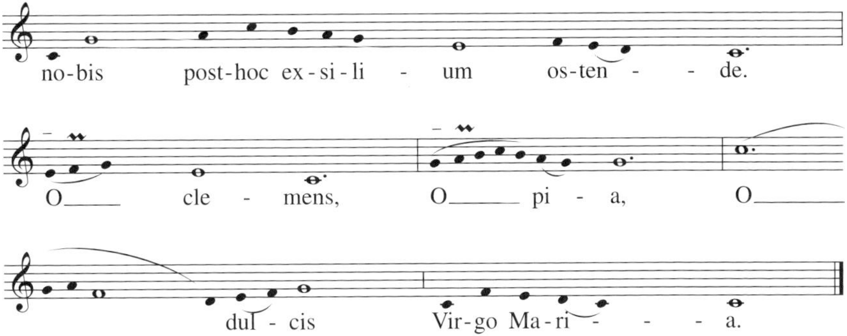

TEXT: traditional Latin

MUSIC: SALVE, REGINA (traditional chant)

Hail, Holy Queen, Enthroned Above

1. Hail, ho - ly Queen, en - throned a - bove. O Ma - ri - a. Hail,
2. Our life, our sweet - ness here be - low, O Ma - ri - a. our
3. To you Eve's child - ren raise their cries, O Ma - ri - a. To
4. From you, most gra - cious ad - vo - cate, O Ma - ri - a, the
5. When this our earth - ly life is done, O Ma - ri - a, show
6. O gen - tle, lov - ing, Vir - gin sweet, O Ma - ri - a. Hail,

moth'r of mer - cy and of love, O Ma - ri - a.
hope in time of trial and woe, O Ma - ri - a.
you they bring both tears and sighs, O Ma - ri - a.
gaze of mer - cy we a - wait, O Ma - ri - a.
un - to us your bless - ed Son, O Ma - ri - a.
Moth'r of God, whom we en - treat, O Ma - ri - a!

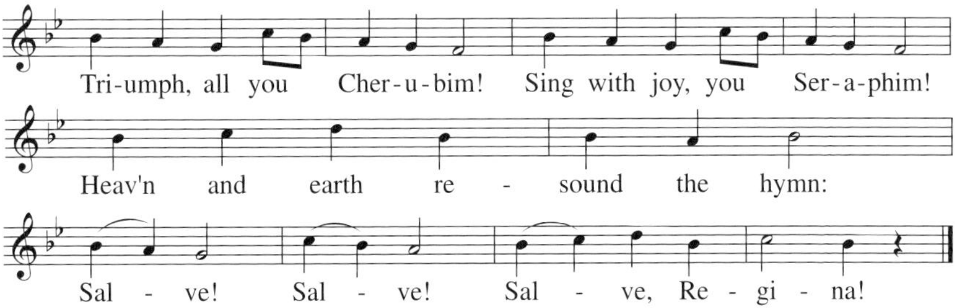

Text: Salve, Regina c. 1080, tr. Roman Hymnal (1884) and Raymond J. Lahey (2002)

Tune: SALVE REGINA CŒLITUM 84.84 with refrain

How to Use This Booklet

This booklet has been designed for both individuals and groups to help them pray the Rosary in the way the Pope has suggested.

The Rosary begins in one of the two familiar ways given here. Then each mystery begins with a reading from Scripture, either the shorter or longer form, and a brief period of reflection. The booklet also provides a phrase to add to each *Hail Mary* for that particular mystery. For the end of each decade, it includes a simple sung version of the *Glory to the Father* and a variety of suitable concluding prayers. (See pp. 19-21.) An evocative line drawing offers you an opportunity to deepen your contemplation of each of the mysteries of Christ.

Individuals may follow the Rosary as it is presented here. Groups that wish to pray the Rosary together may, when there is a choice of readings, use the longer reading noted here or choose one of the other readings listed. Public readings could be done by a person other than the leader. They should begin with "A reading from the Holy Gospel according to ..." and end with the words "The Gospel of the Lord" (response: "Praise to you, Lord Jesus

Christ"). If the reading is not from the Gospels, begin with the words "A reading from the letter of ... to ... [or from the Acts of the Apostles / the book of Revelation]" and end with "The Word of the Lord" (response: "Thanks be to God").

For the end of the Rosary, sung versions of the Latin and English *Hail, Holy Queen* are provided (see pp. 23-26), as is the *Litany of Loreto* (see pp. 76-78). These may be copied for distribution to those who take part.

The Joyful Mysteries

The Annunciation

The angel said to her, "Do not be afraid, Mary, for you have found favour with God. And now, you will conceive in your womb and bear a son, and you will name him Jesus. He will be great, and will be called the Son of the Most High."

(Luke 1.30-32; longer reading is Luke 1.26-38.)

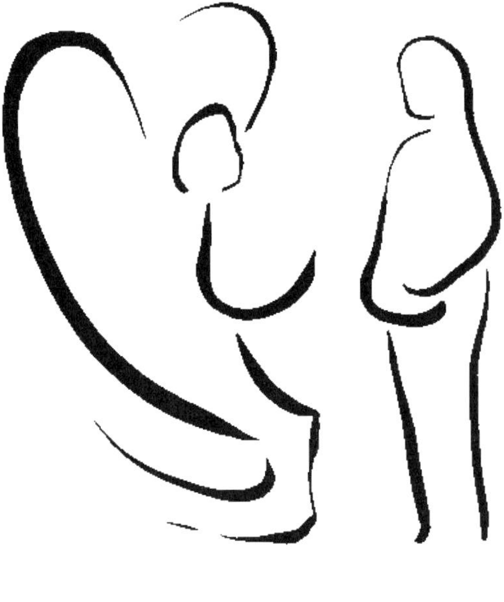

"...the fruit of your womb, Jesus,
whose birth was foretold
by the message of an angel."

The Visitation

Elizabeth was filled with the Holy Spirit and exclaimed with a loud cry, "Blessed are you among women, and blessed is the fruit of your womb."

(Luke 1.41-42; longer reading is Luke 1:39-56.)

"...the fruit of your womb, Jesus,
whose blessedness
Elizabeth first proclaimed."

The Birth of Jesus, the Lord

The angel said to them: … "I am bringing you good news of great joy for all the people: to you is born this day in the city of David a Saviour, who is Christ the Lord."

Luke 2.10-11; longer reading is Luke 2:1-20. See also Matthew 1.18-25; John 1.1-18.)

"...the fruit of your womb, Jesus,
the Word made flesh,
who dwelt among us."

The Presentation in the Temple

Simeon took the child Jesus in his arms and praised God, saying, "My eyes have seen your salvation, which you have prepared in the presence of all peoples."

(Luke 2.28-30; longer reading is Luke 2.22-40.)

"...the fruit of your womb, Jesus,
who is the light of all the nations."

The Finding in the Temple

After three days they found Jesus in the temple, sitting among the teachers, listening to them and asking them questions. And all who heard him were amazed at his understanding and his answers.

(Luke 2.46-47; longer reading is Luke 2.41-52.)

"...the fruit of your womb, Jesus,
who did the work of his Father."

The Mysteries of Light

The Baptism of Jesus in the Jordan

And just as Jesus was coming up out of the water, he saw the heavens torn apart and the Spirit descending like a dove on him. And a voice came from heaven, "You are my Son, the Beloved; with you I am well pleased."

(Mark 1.10-11; longer reading is Mark 1.1-11. See also Matthew 3.13-17; John 1.29-34.)

"...the fruit of your womb, Jesus,
who was baptized by John
and anointed with the Spirit."

The Wedding Feast of Cana

Jesus did this, the first of
his signs, in Cana of Galilee,
and revealed his glory;
and his disciples believed in him.

(John 2.11; longer reading is
John 2.1-11.)

"...the fruit of your womb, Jesus,
who at Cana revealed his glory."

The Proclamation of the Kingdom of God

Jesus came to Galilee, proclaiming the good news of God, and saying, "The time is fulfilled, and the kingdom of God has come near; repent, and believe in the good news."

(Mark 1.14-15.
See also Mark 2.3-13;
Matthew 4.12-17.)

"...the fruit of your womb, Jesus,
who proclaimed the Good News of salvation."

The Transfiguration

While he was praying, the appearance of his face changed, and his clothes became dazzling white. … And from the cloud came a voice that said: "This is my Son, my Chosen; listen to him!"

(Luke 9.29, 35; longer reading is Luke 9.28-36. See also Mark 9.2-10; 2 Peter 1.16-18.)

*"...the fruit of your womb, Jesus,
who was transfigured on the holy mountain."*

The Institution of the Eucharist

While they were eating, Jesus took a loaf of bread, and after blessing it he broke it, gave it to the disciples, and said, "Take, eat; this is my body." Then he took a cup, and after giving thanks he gave it to them, saying, "Drink from it, all of you; for this is my blood of the covenant, which is poured out for many for the forgiveness of sins."

(Matthew 26.26-28; longer reading is Matthew 26.26-29. See also 1 Corinthians 11.23-26; John 6.52-59.)

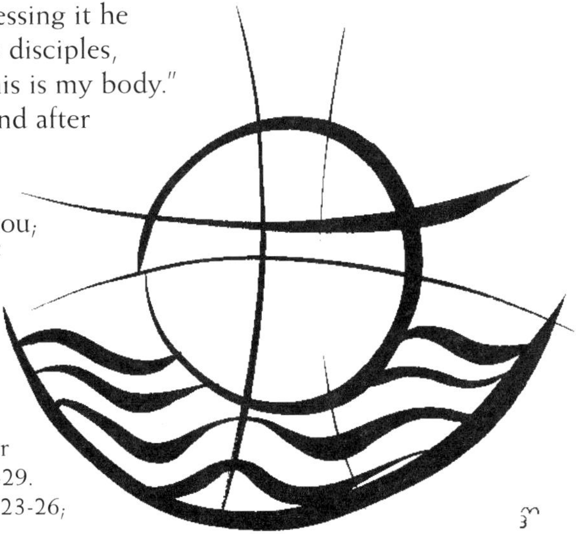

"…the fruit of your womb, Jesus,
who gave us his body and blood."

The Sorrowful Mysteries

The Agony in the Garden

Then Jesus withdrew from them about a stone's throw, knelt down, and prayed, "Father, if you are willing, remove this cup from me; yet, not my will but yours be done."

(Luke 22.41-42; longer reading is Luke 22.39-46. See also Matthew 26.36-46.)

*"...the fruit of your womb, Jesus,
who did the will of the Father."*

The Scourging at the Pillar

So Pilate, wishing to satisfy the crowd, released Barabbas for them; and after flogging Jesus, he handed him over to be crucified.

(Mark 15.15; longer reading is Mark 15.6-15. See also Matthew 27.24-26.)

"...the fruit of your womb, Jesus,
by whose wounds we are healed."

The Crowning with Thorns

The soldiers clothed him in a purple cloak; and after twisting some thorns into a crown, they put it on him. And they began saluting him: "Hail, King of the Jews!"

(Mark 15.17-18; longer reading is Mark 15.16-21. See also Matthew 27.27-31; John 19.2-7.)

"...the fruit of your womb, Jesus,
in whom the kingdom of God draws near."

Carrying of the Cross

Then Jesus said to them all,
"If any want to become
my followers, let them
deny themselves
and take up their
cross daily
and follow me."

(Luke 9.23; longer reading
is Luke 9.21-27.
See also Luke 23.26-33;
1 Corinthians 1.17-25.)

"...the fruit of your womb, Jesus, who by his holy cross redeemed the world."

The Lord's Death upon the Cross

And being found in human form, he humbled himself and became obedient to the point of death—even death on a cross. Therefore God also highly exalted him, and gave him the name that is above every name.

(Philippians 2.8-9; longer reading is Philippians 2.5-11. See also John 3.13-17; John 19.16-30.)

"...the fruit of your womb, Jesus,
who died to sin, once for all."

The Glorious Mysteries

The Resurrection of the Lord

We have been buried with him
by baptism into death,
so that, just as Christ
was raised from the dead by
the glory of the Father,
so we too might
walk in newness of life.

(Romans 6.4; longer reading is
Romans 6.3-11. See also
Matthew 28.1-10; Acts 10.36-43.)

"...the fruit of your womb, Jesus,
whom God raised from the dead."

The Ascension into Heaven

So then the Lord Jesus, after he had spoken to them, was taken up into heaven and sat down at the right hand of God. And they went out and proclaimed the good news everywhere.

(Mark 16.19-20; longer reading is Mark 16.15-20. See also Acts 1.6-11.)

"...the fruit of your womb, Jesus,
who ascended into heaven."

The Outpouring of the Holy Spirit

When the day of Pentecost had come, they were all together in one place. And suddenly from heaven there came a sound like the rush of a violent wind, and it filled the entire house where they were sitting. Divided tongues, as of fire, appeared among them, and a tongue rested on each of them. All of them were filled with the Holy Spirit.

(Acts 2.1, 3-4; longer reading is Acts 1.12-14, 2.1-11. See also 1 Corinthians 12.1-13; John 14.15-26.)

"...the fruit of your womb, Jesus,
in whose name was poured out the Holy Spirit."

The Assumption of Mary

And Mary said: …
"Surely, from now on all generations will call me blessed; for the Mighty One has done great things for me, and holy is his name."

(Luke 1.48-49; longer reading is Luke 1.46-55. See also 1 Corinthians 15.20-26; 1 Thessalonians 4.13-18.)

"...the fruit of your womb, Jesus,
whose death is our victory over death."

The Crowning of Mary in Glory

When Jesus saw his mother and the disciple whom he loved standing beside her, he said to his mother: "Woman, here is your son." Then he said to the disciple: "Here is your mother."

(John 19.26; longer reading is John 19.25-27. See also Revelation 19.5-9; Revelation 12.1-5a; Luke 1.46-55.)

"…the fruit of your womb, Jesus,
in whom you have won
an unfading crown of glory."

Litany of Loreto

Lord, have mercy.
Christ, have mercy.
Lord, have mercy.
Christ, hear us.
Christ, graciously hear us.

God the Father of heaven, have mercy on us.
God the Son, Redeemer of the world, have mercy on us.
God the Holy Spirit, have mercy on us.
Holy Trinity, one God, have mercy on us.

Holy Mary, pray for us.
Holy Mother of God, pray for us.
Holy Virgin of virgins, pray for us.
Mother of Christ, pray for us.
Mother of the Church, pray for us.
Mother of divine grace, pray for us.
Mother most pure, pray for us.
Mother most chaste, pray for us.
Mother inviolate, pray for us.
Mother undefiled, pray for us.
Mother most amiable, pray for us.
Mother most admirable, pray for us.
Mother of good counsel, pray for us.
Mother of our Creator, pray for us.
Mother of our Saviour, pray for us.
Mother of Mercy, pray for us.
Virgin most prudent, pray for us.
Virgin most venerable, pray for us.
Virgin most renowned, pray for us.
Virgin most powerful, pray for us.

Virgin most merciful, pray for us.
Virgin most faithful, pray for us.
Mirror of justice, pray for us.
Seat of wisdom, pray for us.
Cause of our joy, pray for us.
Spiritual vessel, pray for us.
Vessel of honour, pray for us.
Singular vessel of devotion, pray for us.
Mystical rose, pray for us.
Tower of David, pray for us.
Tower of ivory, pray for us.
House of gold, pray for us.
Ark of the covenant, pray for us.
Gate of heaven, pray for us.
Morning star, pray for us.
Health of the sick, pray for us.
Refuge of sinners, pray for us.
Comforter of the afflicted, pray for us.
Help of Christians, pray for us.
Queen of angels, pray for us.
Queen of patriarchs, pray for us.
Queen of prophets, pray for us.
Queen of apostles, pray for us.
Queen of martyrs, pray for us.
Queen of confessors, pray for us.
Queen of virgins, pray for us.
Queen of all saints, pray for us.
Queen conceived without original sin, pray for us.
Queen assumed into heaven, pray for us.
Queen of the most holy Rosary, pray for us.
Queen of families, pray for us.
Queen of peace, pray for us.
Lamb of God, who takes away the sins of the world, spare us, O Lord.

Lamb of God, who takes away the sins of the world, graciously hear us, O Lord.
Lamb of God, who takes away the sins of the world, have mercy on us.

V. Pray for us, O holy Mother of God.

R. That we may be made worthy of the promises of Christ.

Let us pray.

Grant, we beseech you, O Lord our God, that we your servants may enjoy lasting health of mind and body, and, by the glorious intercession of the Blessed Mary, ever Virgin, be delivered from present sorrow and enter into the joy of eternal happiness.
Through Christ Our Lord.

R. Amen.

Notes

1 Stephan Tobler, "Rosary May Contribute to Unity, Says Protestant Theologian, If Contemplated as a Christological Prayer, as Suggested by Pope," Zenit News Agency, December 12, 2002.

2 Some people have referred to these new mysteries as "Luminous Mysteries." However, here they are referred to as "Mysteries of Light," since this is the term used in the Vatican's official English translation of the Pope's letter. This is a faithful translation of the Latin text, which calls them "*lucis mysteria*." Moreover, in referring to the other sets of mysteries, the Latin text has similar wording, so that John Paul II also uses for the other mysteries slightly new titles: "Mysteries of Joy," "Mysteries of Sorrow," and "Mysteries of Glory."

3 In instituting these new mysteries, Pope John Paul II approved and adapted a suggestion made in 1957 by a Maltese priest whom he beatified in 2001. It was Blessed George Preca (1880–1962) who first proposed a set of Mysteries of Light similar to those John Paul II eventually endorsed: the Baptism of the Lord, his miracles, the teaching of the beatitudes, the transfiguration and the Last Supper.

4 Another approved version of the Our Father, from the English Language Liturgical Consultation, is as follows:
Our Father in heaven, hallowed be your name; your kingdom come, your will be done, on earth as in heaven. Give us today our daily bread. Forgive us our sins as we forgive those who sin against us. Save us from the time of trial and deliver us from evil. Amen.

5 From the *Collection of Masses of the Blessed Virgin Mary*, issued by the Holy See in 1988.

6 From the *Collection of Masses of the Blessed Virgin Mary*.

7 From the *Collection of Masses of the Blessed Virgin Mary*.

8 From the *Collection of Masses of the Blessed Virgin Mary*.

9 Lists of the Pope's general and mission intentions are available in the *Living with Christ* yearly missal published by Novalis: 1-877-702-7773.